A DINOSAUR ALPHABET

The of Prehistoric Beasts!

by Michelle Hasselius

illustrated by Clair Rossiter

raintree

a Capstone company — publishers for children

A is for Ankylosaurus.

Ankylosaurus swung its heavy club tail at hungry predators like Tyrannosaurus rex. **BAM!** The strong armour on Ankylosaurus's skin protected it from sharp teeth and claws.

(ANG-kuh-lo-SAWR-us)

B is for Brachiosaurus.

Brachiosaurus was **BIG!** It was taller than the trees!
This giant dino was one of the largest animals ever to walk on Earth.

(BRACK-ee-uh-SAWR-us)

3

is for Coelophysis.

Coelophysis was a small, speedy dinosaur. It weighed about as much as a border collie. The dinosaur could chase after tasty lizards or run away from predators.

(SEE-lo-FY-sis)

D is for Dracorex.

Dracorex looked like a spiky-headed dragon. The dinosaur's full name means "dragon king of Hogwarts". It was named after Hogwarts School in the Harry Potter books.

(DRAY-co-rex)

E is for Euoplocephalus.

Euoplocephalus was ready for battle! It had sharp spikes down its back and armour on its head and body. Euoplocephalus even had armour on its eyelids!

(YOU-oh-plo-SEF-ah-lus)

F is for Futalognkosaurus.

Futalognkosaurus was a very *loooong* dinosaur. It measured 30 metres (100 feet) from its tail to its head. That's longer than a basketball court.

(FOO-tah-lon-koh-SAWR-us)

G is for Gallimimus.

Gallimimus could really go! The dashing dinosaur could run up to 48 kilometres (30 miles) per hour. That's as fast as a tiger can run today. **Zoom!**

(GAL-ih-MY-mus)

H is for Huayangosaurus.

Huayangosaurus was one of the first stegosaurs. It was much smaller than its famous relative, Stegosaurus.

(hwi-YANG-uh-SAWR-us)

I is for Iguanodon.

Iguanodon had five fingers on each front foot. But they didn't look like your fingers. The dinosaur's three middle fingers were stuck together. Instead of thumbs, Iguanodon had long, sharp spikes.

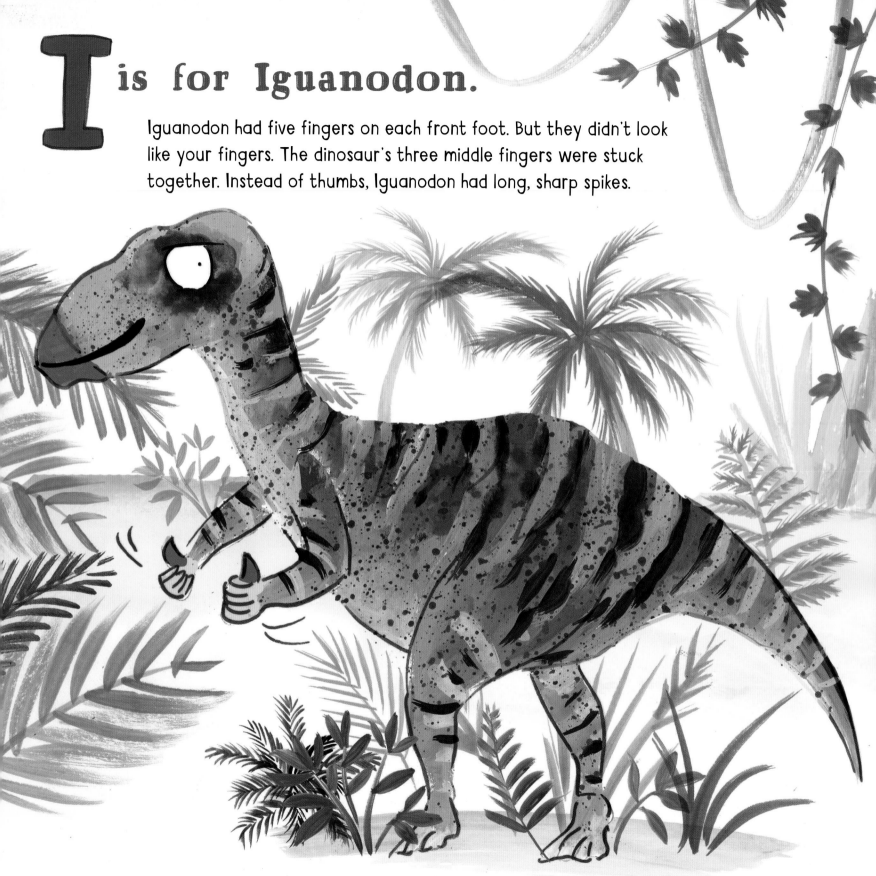

(ih-GWAN-oh-dahn)

10

J is for Janenschia.

Janenschia was a giant plant-eating dinosaur. It used its long neck to pluck the leaves off the tops of tall trees.

(ja-NEN-she-ah)

K is for Kentrosaurus.

Kentrosaurus was a stegosaur, like Huayangosaurus. Kentrosaurus had two rows of strong plates that went halfway down its back. Then the plates turned to spikes, which ran down its tail.

(KEN-tro-SAWR-us)

L is for Leptoceratops.

Leptoceratops was a member of the horned dinosaurs. It and some of the other "horned" dinosaurs didn't actually have horns. Leptoceratops had a frill on its head.

(LEP-tuh-SER-uh-tops)

M is for Megalosaurus.

Megalosaurus was a big meat-eater that walked on two legs. Its sharp, jagged teeth looked like a saw. Megalosaurus was one of the first dinosaurs ever discovered.

(MEG-ah-lo-SAWR-us)

N is for Neovenator.

Neovenator was a deadly hunter. The dinosaur had three sharp claws on each foot. It chased after dinosaurs and attacked. **Watch out!**

(NEE-oh-vuh-NAY-tur)

O is for Oviraptor.

Oviraptor looked like a bird. It had feathers and a hard beak. But the dinosaur couldn't fly. Instead it ran on its two back legs, like an ostrich.

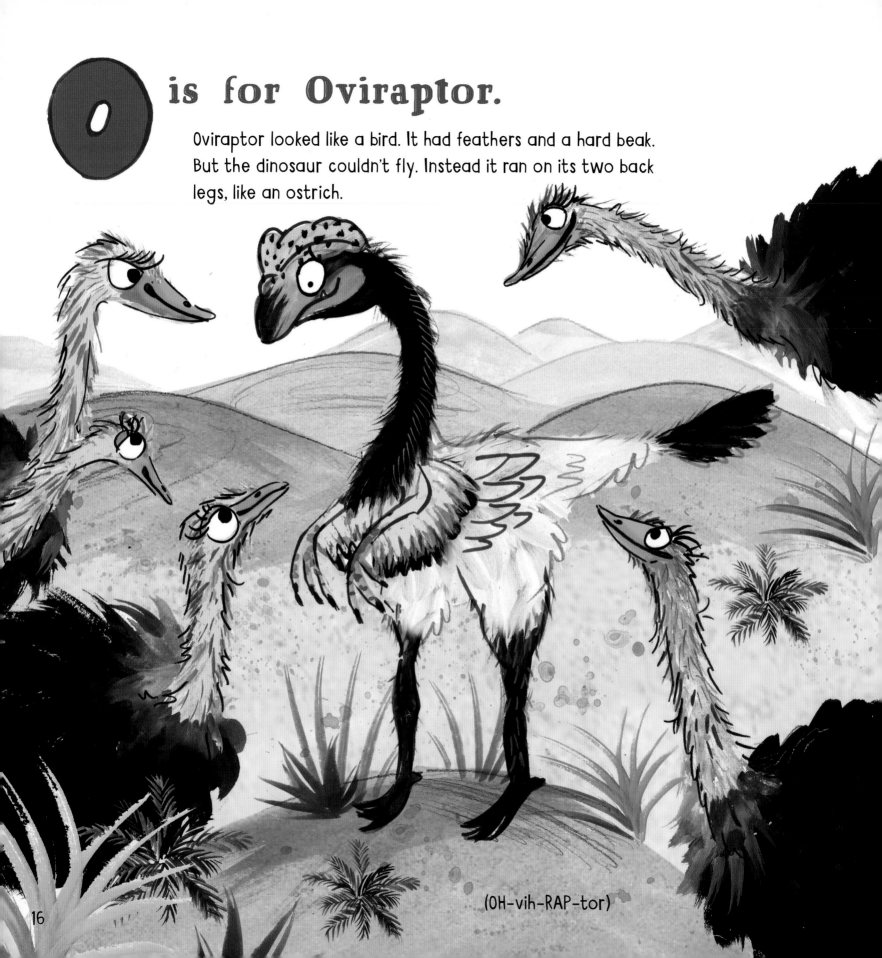

(OH-vih-RAP-tor)

P is for Protoceratops.

Protoceratops had a sharp beak and bony frill. Fossils from this and another dinosaur, Velociraptor, were found in Mongolia. Scientists think they were in the middle of a battle when a sandstorm covered them both with sand.

(PRO-to-SER-uh-tops)

is for Qianzhousaurus.

Qianzhousaurus was a carnivore with a long snout. It was so long and pointed, scientists call this dinosaur "Pinocchio Rex."

(shee-AHN-zhoo-SAWR-us)

18

R is for Rajasaurus.

Rajasaurus's name means "prince lizard". This meat-eater didn't live in a castle. Rajasaurus did have a small crest on its head that looked like a crown.

(RAH-jah-SAWR-us)

S is for **Stegosaurus.**

Stegosaurus is the most well-known stegosaur. Stegosaurus's brain was the size of a walnut, but its body was as big as a bus!

(STEG-uh-SAWR-us)

T is for Tyrannosaurus rex.

Tyrannosaurus rex may be the most popular dinosaur. It had a huge head full of razor-sharp teeth. Scientists think the dinosaur could eat up to 227 kilograms (500 pounds) of meat in one bite. **Chomp!**

(ty-RAN-uh-SAWR-us REX)

U is for Utahraptor.

Utahraptor is the biggest raptor discovered so far. It had a deadly, 23-centimetre (9-inch) claw on each foot. This hunter sunk its claw into even bigger dinosaurs, like Iguanodon.

(YU-tah-RAP-tor)

V is for Velociraptor.

Velociraptor was about the size of a small turkey. Even though it was small, the raptor was dangerous. Velociraptor had sharp teeth and a curved claw on each foot. Velociraptor may have even hunted in packs to kill larger dinosaurs.

(vuh-LOSS-uh-RAP-tor)

23

W is for Wuerhosaurus.

Wuerhosaurus was one of the last stegosaurs on Earth.
It lived in Asia more than 110 million years ago.

(woo-EHR-ho-SAWR-us)

X is for Xenoceratops.

Xenoceratops's name means "alien horned face". But it's not from another world. This big dinosaur had two long horns over its eyes and little horns all around its frill.

(ZEE-no-SER-uh-tops)

Y is for Yi qi.

Yi qi was about the size of a pigeon. It had wings like a bat, but it couldn't fly. Instead the dinosaur glided through the air.

(EE CHEE)

26

Z is for Zhongyuansaurus.

Zhongyuansaurus was the only ankylosaur that didn't have a club tail. But it could still protect itself with its hard armour.

(ZHONG-yu-an-SAWR-us)

Glossary

ankylosaur group of plant-eating dinosaurs from the Cretaceous Period with thick bodies and bony armour; Ankylosaurus was an ankylosaur

armour bones, scales and skin that some animals have on their bodies for protection

beak hard front part of a bird's mouth; some dinosaurs had beaks

carnivore animal that eats only meat

fossil remains or traces of an animal or plant from millions of years ago, preserved in rock

frill large, bony plate that grows from the back of an animal's skull

glide move through the air in a controlled way but without power

herbivore animal that eats only plants

plate flat, bony growth on an animal

predator animal that hunts other animals for food

sandstorm strong windstorm that blows sand around

snout long front part of an animal's head; the snout includes the nose, mouth and jaws

spike sharp, pointy part of an animal

stegosaur group of plant-eating dinosaurs that walked on four legs and had plates and spikes on their bodies; Stegosaurus was a stegosaur

Read More

Alphasaurs and Other Prehistoric Types, Sharon Werner and Sarah Forss (Blue Apple Books, 2013)

I Learn with Dinosaurs, David West (Crabtree, 2013)

Pop-Up Dinosaur Alphabet, Robert Crowther (Walker Books, 2014).

Websites

www.kidsdinos.com
Learn about dinosaurs with information, games and activities.

www.nhm.ac.uk/discover/dino-directory/index.html
The Natural History's Museum's online guide to dinosaurs, with images, facts and figures for more than 300 dinosaurs.

Index

Raintree is an imprint of Capstone Global Library Limited, a company incorporated
in England and Wales having its registered office at 264 Banbury Road, Oxford, OX2 7DY –
Registered company number: 6695582

www.raintree.co.uk
myorders@raintree.co.uk

Text © Capstone Global Library Limited 2017
The moral rights of the proprietor have been asserted.

Editor: Gillia Olson
Designer: Ashlee Suker
Art Director: Nathan Gassman
Production Specialist: Katy LaVigne
The illustrations in this book were created digitally.

ISBN 978 1 4747 2442 5
20 19 18 17 16
10 9 8 7 6 5 4 3 2 1

British Library Cataloguing in Publication Data
A full catalogue record for this book is available from the British Library.

Every effort has been made to contact copyright holders of material reproduced in this book. Any
omissions will be rectified in subsequent printings if notice is given to the publisher.

All the Internet addresses (URLs) given in this book were valid at the time of going to press.
However, due to the dynamic nature of the Internet, some addresses may have changed, or sites
may have changed or ceased to exist since publication. While the author and publisher regret any
inconvenience this may cause readers, no responsibility for any such changes can be accepted by
either the author or the publisher.

Printed and Bound in China.

Other Titles in this Series